Yevtushenko

SELECTED POEMS

TRANSLATED WITH AN INTRODUCTION
BY ROBIN MILNER-GULLAND
AND PETER LEVI, S. J.

E. P. DUTTON & CO., INC.
NEW YORK: 1962

First published in the United States, 1962,
simultaneously by E. P. Dutton & Co., Inc.
and Penguin Books

Published simultaneously in Canada by
Clarke, Irwin & Company Limited,
Toronto and Vancouver

Library of Congress Catalog Card Number: 62-20476

First Printing September 1962
Second Printing January 1963
Third Printing March 1964

Contents

Introduction

IT would be unrewarding to attempt in this introduction any very detailed analysis of Yevtushenko's antecedents and of hypothetical formative influences on him. But it seems appropriate to give a brief outline of the general framework of Soviet Russian literature, then of his life, work, and place in this framework, before looking at his own poems and the problems of translating them.

There have been two periods notable above any others for a flowering of Russian poetry. The first, associated with the names of Pushkin and Lermontov, falls roughly within the dates 1810–40; the second occupies the first three decades of the present century. The latter period is one of particular importance in the development of Soviet literature. It spans the years on either side of the Revolution and was an age of unrivalled variety and experiment. Though a succession of poetic schools held sway – Symbolism, Futurism, Acmeism, Constructivism, Imagism – their leading adherents are remarkable for the individuality of their voices, despite these formal labels. What is particularly interesting is that almost without exception the important poets of the age were active writers both before the Revolution and in the Soviet Union after it: Blok, Bryusov, Pasternak, Mayakovsky, Akhmatova, Mandelshtam, Bagritsky, Khlebnikov, Yesenin all come into this category. Each of them accepted the Revolution and the demands of the young Soviet state in his own way, and the differing reactions produced in these writers by the new order of society form a moving and absorbing study.

After this flying start the second phase of Soviet poetry

7

must seem somewhat of an anticlimax. By the end of 1934 all the poets listed above had died save Akhmatova, Mandelshtam, and Pasternak; and even these three published no original verse during the thirties. During that decade stricter government control over literature discouraged the exuberant experimentation characteristic of previous years. Not that literature was altogether at a low ebb after the twenties, for good novels were being written; but for some reason – as in the second half of the nineteenth century — an era of good prose-writing coincided with a leàn patch in poetry. Particularly unfortunate was the dearth of new poets, brought up in the Soviet state, who might have replaced the disappearing pioneers of Soviet literature. (Right up to the present decade this lack has been noticeable, and the leading Soviet writers have continued to be largely those who grew up before 1917.) But poetry does not simply die out, and from the late twenties to the forties a certain number of talented poets did begin to publish: Zabolotsky, Tvardovsky, Margarita Aliger. During the war a good deal more verse was published than previously (both by new writers and by ones who had been silent for some time) and its quality seemed to presage a revival. But by 1948 the stern directives of Zhdanov, the Minister of Culture, made it clear that the outlook for imaginative poets was no more favourable than in the thirties. For the rest of Stalin's lifetime poetic activity was almost at a standstill.

The last years of Stalin coincide with the earliest publications of a very young writer, Yevgeny Alexandrovich Yevtushenko. He had been born in 1933, long after the Revolution, the Civil War, the death of Lenin; the tense emotions of those years, or even of the Second World War, could not serve as a first-hand inspiration to him as they had done to most of the good Soviet poetry which was not of a purely lyrical nature. In Yevtushenko, born and brought up in an already securely established Soviet Union, there could be no question of an inner conflict between the attractions of the old order of society and the new, whose resolution was of such vital importance to the poets of the first era after the Revolution. The remarkable impact that Yevtushenko made sprang more than anything else from his being the representative of a quite new generation, seeing old truths through fresh eyes as each new generation must. By consistently refusing to compromise his regard for truth or his concept of good poetry he became this new generation's unchallenged literary spokesman, and opened a way for the host of talented young poets that has emerged in the last decade.

When asked about his early life, Yevtushenko is apt to refer the questioner to his poetry; this is indeed so autobiographical that one can learn almost everything important about the writer from it. He was born in the remote town of Zima on the trans-Siberian railway, of mixed Ukrainian, Russian, and Tartar blood, in a peasant family. 'Zima Junction' vividly describes his childhood in Siberia and his return there at the age of twenty after a long absence in Moscow. His father was a geologist, and when only fifteen and seventeen years old he took part himself in geological expeditions to Kazakhstan and to the Altai. He was a considerable athlete: cycling, ping-pong, football (he was a goal-keeper) were among his favourite activities, and his first published poems were actually printed in a sporting journal in 1949. The seeds of his poetic talent had, however, been sown some time earlier, when as a child during the war he had been made to dance and sing – and found himself improvising verses. It is interesting that some of his more recent poems, though not intended specifically as songs, have been set to music and have become extremely popular in this form.

He was accepted as a student by the Moscow Literary Institute, where he achieved little success. Though he had been writing from an early age, his poetic talent took some time to mature. His first book of poems was published in 1952; his second, *Third Snow* (*Trety sneg*, 1955), contains two of the earliest poems of his that appear in the present volume ('Lies', 'The Companion'). Shortly afterwards ensued a period of brilliant work. The years 1955–7 mark a peak of quality in his poetry; from 1956 alone date 'Zima Junction' and no less than six of the shorter poems in our collection. It was a prolific period – books of his verse appeared in 1955, 1956, and 1957, each better than the one before. But new-found fame and popularity had its dangers. Many Soviet literary critics, themselves relics of the deadening last years of Stalin when poetry was almost completely stifled by political dogmatism, reacted with violent hostility to the appearance of a fresh, talented, unashamedly self-confident young poet whose professed concern was to seek out truth for himself and not to have it dictated to him from above. From that time to the present he has been the subject of many hostile articles in literary journals (for example in *Komsomolskaya Pravda* of 21 June 1957, *Literaturnaya Gazeta* of 8 April 1958, *Literatura i Zhizn* of 27 November 1961); after the publication of 'Zima Junction' he had to withdraw temporarily from the Komsomol organization. But it would be quite wrong to make Yevtushenko out to be a victim of unrelenting persecution; one can also point to enthusiastic articles (e.g. in *Novy Mir*, 1957:5, and in *Literaturnaya Gazeta*, 9 January 1960). The Soviet Union is a more complex place than the West seems prepared to believe, and particularly in the literary world (where ceaseless and often fruitful controversy is carried on between highly disparate factions); to speak of any monolithic 'party line' and to try and measure a writer against it is senseless.

In 1959 Yevtushenko produced two books. *Longbow and Lyre* (*Luk i Lira*) contains original poems about Georgia and many translations from the Georgian language. *Poems of Several Years* (*Stikhi Raznykh Let*) is a retrospective anthology of his work, containing most of his best shorter poems and a sequel to 'Zima Junction' titled 'Where are you from?' – much less aesthetically satisfying than its predecessor but with some interesting passages. The edition was of 20,000 copies, and of course sold out immediately. Yevtushenko's next book of new poems, *The Apple* (*Yabloko*), came out a year or so later, and at first sight seemed a disappointment; it contains only one or two of his best poems (e.g. 'Birthday', 'Colours'). But it does display in many otherwise unremarkable poems a development in the poet's style. Less dramatic, denser, more reflective, these poems lack the sparkle (and the occasionally facile optimism) of his youthful work and they seem in fact to have led to a new flowering of his talent in the last couple of years. Such work as 'Babiy Yar' and 'People' shows that his inspiration has by no means dried up in his late twenties, as has so often happened to prolific poets.

Various things may have contributed to this new upsurge in Yevtushenko's poetry. Since 1960 he has travelled abroad a great deal; to France, Africa, the United States, Cuba, Great Britain. Insatiably curious, open-minded, with an enormous appetite for people, he has found foreign travel enriching to him as a poet and a person, just as earlier he found excitement and inspiration in the trans-caucasian Republic of Georgia. An equally potent inspiration has been his second, happier marriage to Galina Semyonovna, a fellow-Siberian (his first, to the brilliant poetess Bella Akhmadulina, dated from 1954). His most recent book (*Vzmakh Ruki*, 1962) contains a better selection of his work than any previous anthology, together with some of his powerful recent work. It came out with a spectacular printing of 100,000 copies, showing that (as he says himself) nowadays at last the publication of a Soviet poet is determined by the demands of the reading public rather than his place in any official hierarchy. His activity is remarkable. Apart from his large output of verse he has experimented with prose-writing and, currently, film-making; at the same time he is in enormous demand to recite his published and unpublished poetry in Russian clubs, factories, universities, and theatres – he claims to have made about 250 such readings in 1961.

How does this poetry compare with that of his Soviet predecessors? Though fresh, it is not strikingly innovatory, and he owes a good deal to the past. It could tentatively be described as middlebrow poetry, and as such it lacks the obscurity associated with Khlebnikov and other early twentieth-century writers. Among modern poets his greatest admiration is for Blok, Mayakovsky, Yesenin, and Pasternak (whom he knew personally). He has most in common with Mayakovsky and Yesenin. Like Mayakovsky, he is by temperament a natural revolutionary, hating stagnation, bondage, hypocrisy – and with a fundamentally gentle nature, unpuritanical and libertarian, insistent that ends do not justify bad means. He owes much to Mayakovsky stylistically, above all the declamatory, powerful, colloquial aspects of his verse, whose impact often cannot be fully appreciated until it is heard aloud. Like Yesenin, he is a peasant boy who has come to the city – and for whom his remote birthplace continues to hold a deeply felt significance; vigorously sensual, often regarded by his elders as a destructive and degenerate influence (though in reality a passionate seeker after truth and moral justice). But Yevtushenko is an original poet, and cannot be fully characterized by his antecedents alone, any more than the numerous young poets now writing in the Soviet Union are to be characterized simply by reference to Yevtushenko (who nevertheless has blazed the trail for them). His work as a whole shows a fundamental feature which is typical of the best Russian poetry since early in the last century: an ability to move effortlessly from social to personal themes, from the publicistic to the lyrical, to combine them in a single poem. English writers could learn much from him in this.

In this book the translators wish to make available to readers some of the work of a notable living Russian poet, in English versions which aim to be poetry in their own right. Since these – like all translations – must attempt to reconcile two often disparate canons of interpretation (the literal and the literary) they cannot claim to be in any sense perfect or definitive. But we do believe that by preferring in general to produce versions that may make sense as English poetry (even where this has meant abandoning an exact imitation of the rhythm, rhyme, or metaphor of the original) we are likely to present the non-Russian-speaking reader with something more worthwhile than the most painstaking crib. In so doing we have of course tried to keep as close as possible to the original sequence of ideas, without additions or subtractions (which would be unpardonable).

To come suddenly a few years ago on a young Soviet poet of this importance, and to recognize his quality, was a great shock and excitement, particularly for the one of us who knew no Russian, and, for whom a new and wonderful writer was taking an English shape at the end of his pen. Although these translations were made by a poet who knows no Russian and a student of Russian who is not a poet, both translators are of course fully responsible for every part of the final version. The student of Russian sent a word-for-word translation of the passages he selected to the poet, usually with some notes and variants. This was then worked through until a poem in English was produced from it, which was checked and queried and overhauled by each of us alternately, working alone. There were one or two meetings necessary before each piece was settled.

We are both conscious of a distortion which Yevtushenko's poetry has undergone, but there are no lines from which either of us would wish to dissociate himself. It may be possible to give some indications of what the qualities are which we feel have here and there been attenuated or suppressed.

In the first place the originals have a far greater variety of tone and language than these versions. Even the rhythms of 'Zima Junction', which range from those of folk-song to Mayakovskyan sprung verse, and give a continuous impulse of life and at the same time a sense of technical daring to the Russian poem, have had to be damped down. It was simply not possible to reproduce them. The same goes for Yevtushenko's fascinating variety of style. It was not just that there was only a single tone in which we could translate, but that many of the notes open to him in Russian are extremely difficult to play in English poetry today.

Unfortunately it was the extremes that suffered. The most highly rhythmic passages became a little less so, since a rhythm of such intensity in English involves one in lyrics like those of Byron. The colloquialisms at another extreme had to be built into an English context where a sudden verbal shock would have smelt not of life, but of literature. Sublimity of language in Russian and in English makes quite different demands. Our worst sin has probably been to impose a sort of filter on the sparkling and many-sided vitality of the originals.

But it ought still to be possible to grasp in translation some of the interest and particular quality of this poet, which has as much of importance in it for the West perhaps as for his own country. We have no tradition of this sort of writing, and not only is the personal sensibility expressed in these lines quite different from those of the writers we were reared with, but the whole conception and structure of such poetry and the bone on which it grew are somehow outside our experience. In a poem – sensitive to place – about life in contemporary Siberia, this was to be expected. But the very wide area of that life which the poem illuminates, and the direct realism with which so much of it is treated, are more astonishing than any difference of geography or language could account for.

The imaginative core of Yevtushenko's work is in an acceptance of life, a hopefulness, and an honesty, which are directly related to the variety of his surface textures. The first quality of the poet as narrator is youth, and in 'Zima Junction' youth itself comes near to being the subject of the poem. The narrator looks at the external world with direct-ness, at nature with fascination, and at social and industrial circumstances with curiosity, but at the same time his eyes are the introspective and analytic eyes of the young.

The central stronghold of the poems is a rock-like absolute of integrity. In several of the shorter poems this tough moral quality is taken as pre-existent and inalienable, once or twice ruefully, but more often proudly. Perhaps it gets a context in ordinary life from the sort of people the poet admires: his uncles, Andrei and Volodya, in 'Zima Junction', for example, and the strongly stylized image of Hemingway in 'Encounter'. But in several passages of his longer poem 'On a Bicycle', this extreme of independence is treated with detachment and subjected, like other characteristics, to the prolonged self-analysis of youth.

The whole of Yevtushenko's life is at stake in this inquiry and therefore also his belief in the society in which he lives, and in the source of his poems. Since everything stands or falls together in his writing, his fundamental realism about experience involves him at the same time (like Wordsworth in a different tradition and an almost opposite context) in an entire galaxy of accurately observed *sensibilia*, which he records with a tension that expresses his own solitude and tension, and in a searching humanist inquiry into Russian society. This combination of intimate moral stature with an implacable public voice and the attractive personal mannerisms of a likeable poet works itself out in differing proportions in different poems, but it is always present.

These are the factors that infuse poetry directly concerned with everyday life with an intensity of original thought and feeling. Yevtushenko's originality chiefly consists in the position of directly reported life in what he writes about; but it would be difficult finally to estimate any part of his work without reference to the most general and

in fact the most controversial principles. The writer of the
fierce lines against anti-semitism and against time-servers,
the poet of the most solemn passages of 'Zima Junction',
and the young writer so deeply involved by his eagerness
and his sensibility in the powerful imagery of existence,
are each of them a necessary part of the others. His authority as a poet is indivisible. His voice is not stiff and his
gestures are not wooden. The gentle ironies of 'School-
master', the dash, the humour, and the exact light and
shade of 'On a Bicycle', are as essentially connected as his
gravest statements with the quality of hope, with his belief
in the Russian future, his affirmation of the values of life.

Yevtushenko's recent visit to England, on the invitation
of the British Council, forms a curious postscript to this
account of his life and work. Suddenly and quite unex-
pectedly transformed into a celebrity, he was the centre of
much curiosity and an amazing amount of ill-informed
comment.

During the last decade Yevtushenko's poetry had been
more and more talked about in the West, without becom-
ing at all accurately or widely known. This was partly due
to the dying away of serious Western interest in Soviet
writers during the last years of Stalin and the first of the
Cold War; to some extent (in England at least) because of
the extreme narrowness of our literary horizons; and partly
because Soviet poetry had been relayed to us chiefly by
political commentators whose interests were not primarily
literary. And so now the newspapers, having set up
Yevtushenko as Russia's Angry Young Poet, wasted a good
deal of space in knocking down this Aunt Sally of their
own making. In its efforts to categorize him neatly, the
Press cast Yevtushenko in a bewildering variety of roles,

from stalking-horse of the Soviet government to anti-Communist rebel. His clothes, his looks, his habits, his political significance, his place in Soviet society, were all exhaustively described. What received little comment were his character and his poetry, which is perhaps because few had bothered to acquaint themselves with either. It is interesting to see how completely Yevtushenko's poetry contradicts what is generally expected of it, and how many of the commonplaces of what is sometimes dismissed as literature of propaganda exist in this young writer as poetry of the first order. If these translations and this introduction succeed in focusing attention on Yevtushenko's life and work rather than on superficialities, if they can help to strip the arbitrary labels from him which are attached in this country to all things Russian, they will have been worth while.

PETER LEVI, S.J.
ROBIN MILNER-GULLAND

Yevtushenko

SELECTED POEMS

Zima Junction

As we get older we get honester,
that's something.
And these objective changes correspond
like a language to me and my mutations.
If the way I see you now is not the way
in which we saw you once, if in you
what I see now is new
it was by self-discovery I found it.
I realize that my twenty years might be
less than mature: but for a reassessment:
what I said and ought not to have said,
and ought to have said and was silent.

My life has often been by backward glances,
few personal emotions, thoughts or wishes,
and in my life, its even turns and courses,
some generous impulse but nothing finished.
Yet always here these means for a new design,
new strength, touching the same ground
where you first moved bare-footed, kicking up dust.
I rely often on this ordinary thought:
near Lake Baikal my own town waiting for me.

And the wish to see the pines again,
mute witnesses of time and its distance,
of my great-grandfather and of the others
in exile here after a peasant's rising.
Here herded from the extremities of distance
through mud and rain with small children and wives

Ukranian peasants from Zhitomir province.
The trees had spiders' webs.
In wanderings finding fortitude to forget
what each of them loved more than his life.
The guards looked with uneasy eyes
at hands heavy with veins, and the sergeant
sat playing by fire-light: clubs were trumps.
All the night through my great-grandfather
sat thinking there, and lighted up his pipes
with a fiery coal held in his peasant fingers.
What did he think of?

                      Now it would seem to them
arriving there in an unfamiliar region:
welcomes or threats; God knows what it might be like.
He disbelieved the floated fairy-stories
that simple people lived like princes there,
(when was it that the people lived like princes?)
and disbelieved his sudden thoughts and worries;
whatever happened ploughing and sowing
were bound to be the same where there was soil.
You'll find out when you get there prisoner. March.
Plenty of miles to walk before you get there.
And where is she, Ukraine, mother Ukraine?
Who can find the nightingale
where he sings his early song,
unbroken forest around,
no way to him at all
not walking and not riding,
not walking and not riding,
and not flying,
and not flying.

These willy-nilly peasant colonists
took (I suppose) this foreign countryside
like fate, to each his own unhappiness:
one's stepmother however kind-hearted
not being the same as a mother.
They crumbled its soil in their fingers,
drank its water, and let their children drink,
questioned, understood, possessed,
felt it as earth and tied by blood to them.
Put on again the yoke of destitution,
that bitter-tasting life. No one blames
an old nail sliding into a wall,
it's being hammered with the butt of an axe.
There were so many hardships
anxieties of survival,
however much they bent their labouring backs,
it always turned out not to be them
who ate the bread, it was the bread that ate.
Threshing, reaping, harvesting,
in the fields, in the house, in the barns.
There's truth enough where there's enough bread,
see to the bread and truth sees to itself.
Slow thoughts.
My great-grandfather starved all through his life.
The innumerable badness of those harvests.
This was the truth he dreamed about and not
the truth which happened.

It hadn't much to do with great-grandfather,
there was something new, something of us in it,
in 1919 at nine years old

my mother met it suddenly.
One day that autumn heavy rifle-fire
broke like a storm. Sudden on the hillside
a young man crouching over his horse's neck
with a star on his hat and a cossack hair-tuft,
and over the old and creaking bridge behind him
one thunderous charge of flying cavalry,
then horsemen everywhere,
glitter of quivering sabres in the Junction.

There was something handsome gained in this already
– there were no more raiders when the commissar came,
and something in the comic imitations
of the enemy beside the club-room stove,
and something in that young horseman, the lodger,
frenziedly polishing up his cossack boots.

He fell deeply in love with the schoolmistress,
wandered about beside himself with passion
talking to her about all sorts of subjects,
but mostly about the world, its hydra heads;
and slashing with his theory like a sabre
(or that was what his squadron thought about it)
he valued nothing else except ideas:
bread not at all, to hell with bread.
He said, with his bluster and enthusiasm
(backing it up with fists and with quotations),
that the only thing we had to do was push
the bourgeoisie
                    into the sea.
All the rest was easy, life would be fine.

Get into line. Shake out the banners.
And sing revolutionary Hosannas.
Into the sun and trumpets, carrying flowers.
And the road seemed clear ahead to the Commune.

How could he know, with his Cossack top-knot,
so easily deciding life in advance,
that for us it wasn't going to be so simple;
how know the weight and mass of the complications?

Then one morning of wind, wet underfoot,
he stuffed his oat-bags tight, mounted his horse,
said to the schoolmistress simply,
'Good-bye – we'll see each other again,'
and looked far off, rising high in the stirrups
to where the wind came, smelling of explosions;
and his horse hurtled, hurtled him into the east,
shaking and shaking its beribboned mane.

So years went past, one after the other.
I grew up in the small town
acquiring an affection for the forest
and landscape and the quiet houses.
I grew up
            and at hide-and-seek
uncatchable whatever guard you kept
we peered out from the barn through bullet-holes.
There was war at that time;
Hitler not far from Moscow.
                              And we
– we were children and accepted a lot lightly.

From classroom threats untroubled and forgetful
we tore away out of the school playground
and ran down through fields to the river,
broke open a money-box and ran away
to look for the green mare,
baited our wet hooks.
I used to go fishing, stuck paper kites,
or often wandering by myself bare-headed
sucked at clover, grass polished my sandals,
I know the black acres the yellow hives
the luminous clouds that dropped still lightly stirring
half out of sight behind the immense horizon,
and skirting around outhouses used to listen
for the neighing of their horses, peacefully
and tiredly fell asleep in old hayricks
long darkened by the rain.

I scarcely had one single care in the world,
my life, presenting no big obstacles,
seemed to have few or simple complications –
life solved itself without my contributions.
I had no doubts about harmonious answers
which could and would be given to every question.
But suddenly this felt necessity
of answering these questions for myself.
So I shall go on where I started from,
sudden complexity, self-generated,
disturbed by which I started on this journey.

Into my native forest among those
long-trodden roads I took this complication

to take stock of that old simplicity,
– like bride and groom, a country matchmaking.
So there stood youth and there childhood together,
trying to look into each other's eyes
and each offending, but not equally.
Each wanted the other to start talking.
Childhood spoke first, 'Hullo then.
It's your fault if I hardly recognized you.
Once when I often used to dream about you
I thought you'd be quite different from this.
I'll tell you honestly, you worry me.
You're still in very heavy debt to me.'
So youth asked if childhood would help,
and childhood smiled and promised it would help.
They said good-bye, and, walking attentively,
watching the passers-by and the houses,
I stepped happily, uneasily out
through Zima Junction, that important town.

I worked things out about it in advance
– and just in case – with these alternatives,
if it hadn't got any better then it wouldn't
have got any worse.
Somehow the Corn Exchange had got smaller,
so had the chemist shop, so had the park;
it was as if the whole world were smaller
than it was when I left it.
And it was hard at first among other things
to see the streets hadn't all got shorter,
but I was walking with a longer pace
ranging the town.

Once I lived here as if the place were a flat,
could find whatever I wanted in three seconds,
cupboard or bed, could move here in the dark.
Maybe the circumstances had altered,
– and mine had been too long an absence,
but now I bumped on everything I used
to avoid, now knocked against it awkwardly,
and unfamiliarly they caught my eye:
the tall fence with the obscene inscription,
the drunk slumped against the café wall,
the women quarrelling in the shopping queue.
All right if this were any old place,
but this was here, and where I was born,
where I came home for strength and for courage,
for the truth and truth's well-being.
There was a driver cursing the Town Council,
two cooks were fighting under somebody's laughter
and drowsy audience the big burdocks
listened dustily, never moving an ear.
The wooden legs of beggars banged on cobbles,
a small boy with a stick was chasing a cat. . . .
And purposely at first I didn't go
by the directest way, but then later
I started hurrying.
And this was necessary too.
To have drenched my face in freshness,
as I got near to home, near to the gates,
turning the iron ring.
At once from the very first expostulations,
'He's here!' 'Zhenka!' 'Come and eat something!'
from the first embraces, kisses and reproaches,

'And couldn't you have sent us a telegram?'
from, 'We were just lighting the samovar'
from recollections, 'how many years is it?'
just as I thought, all indecision vanished,
and things became peaceful and full of light.
And anxious Aunt Eliza put forward
the strong proposal I should have a wash
since she knew what those trains were like, she said.
Already tureens and kitchen-implements,
already the table dragged to the living-room,
and passing among the grey-blue onion shoots
I went off for water from the well,
waking the well with a cossack song –
the well kept the smells of my childhood,
the bucket came up bumping on the sides,
the chain was wet and sparkled in the light.
So I from Moscow, I the important guest,
hair damped down, clean-shirted,
sat in a crowd of radiant relations,
centre of questions, glasses, scurryings.
I'd got too weak for the great Siberian dishes
and now despaired at the sight of their abundance.
My aunt said, 'Have another bit of gherkin.
What do they feed you on in Moscow then?
You're eating nothing at all. It isn't decent!
Here, take a dumpling. Have some aubergine.'
My uncle said, 'I expect that Moscow vodka's
what you've got used to; try some of this.
Go on, go on – I do say all the same
it isn't good for you, not at your age.
Who taught you that? Look, down in one gulp!

Well, cheers, and God grant it won't be the last.'

We drank and joked and chattered excitedly,
until my sister suddenly thought to ask me
was I at the Hall of Columns in March,
and everyone grew suddenly serious.
They spoke of the year and the year's gravity,
the events and worries and the long reflections.
Uncle Volodya pushed away his glass.
'Nowadays,' he said, 'we all behave
as if we were a sort of philosopher.
It's the times that we live in. People are thinking.
Where, what, how – the answers don't come running.
Now the doctors have turned out innocent;
well, why should people suffer in that way?
It's an international scandal, of course it is,
and all that bloody Beria, I suppose.'
Speaking, not capable of rhetoric,
of what stirred up the emotions in those days:
'You live in Moscow; things are clearer there:
tell me about it all, explain it to me.'
He took me by the buttons so to speak
and wouldn't be put off by anybody;
he made himself a home-rolled cigarette
and waited for an answer.
                          And I think
that I was right, my uncle all attention
as if the truth and I were personal friends,
to answer peacefully, 'I'll tell you later.'

My bed was in the hay-loft as I wanted,

I lay up there and listened for a long time
to the night. Mouth-organ playing. Dance somewhere.
And there was no one any use to me.
It got colder. Prickly with no mattress.
The quiet loft rustled and stirred about;
and Nicky my young brother tirelessly
kept me from sleep, showed me his torch (foreign)
and carried on his grown-up conversation.
But didn't I know Sinyavsky personally?
Had I *really* never seen a helicopter?
And morning came, and I stretched a bit,
and went to sit on the sacks outside the barn,
while dawn rose in the east and lingered on
the heads of cockerels, their scarlet combs.
Half-lighted mist thinned, a few houses
swam into distance, the long poles
of the bird-houses were pushing themselves
ponderously upwards from the ground,
the cows were moving in sedate processions
along the road, an old cowman was cracking
his routine whip a little. Oh it was all
concordant strength and bodily sanity.
I didn't want to think about anything.
Forgetting breakfast, hearing no reproaches,
and travelling light with pockets full of bread
(so when I used to run truant from school,
so now) I got away to the river,
and made for the old big willow on the bank
getting my feet clogged up in the warm mud,
lying on the sand in shade of its branches.
The water murmured in an even voice.

Tree-trunks swam slowly past
bumping now and then. Distant
hooters were sounding.
Some midges sang their high note.
                            Near by
an oldish railwayman, trousers rolled up,
was standing out on a rock with a fishing-rod.
He was scowling at me: what was I doing there?
If I didn't fish myself why not let him?
He searched my face and came closer and said:
'You can't be – ? but wait a minute!
You can't be Zina Yevtushenko's son?
And there was I ... You won't know who I am!
But God bless you! From Moscow? For the summer?
I'll make myself at home if you don't mind.'
He sat beside me and undid his packet:
a hunk of bread, tomatoes, and some salt.
I got worn out with answering his questions,
there was nothing he didn't want to know:
how much in money was my scholarship worth,
how soon would the Exhibition open again?
He was a prickly obstinate old fellow,
and had some sharp-pointed remarks to make,
the young being nothing now to the old days,
and the komsomol so boring it was a pain.
'I remember when your mother was seventeen,
the lads, they used to be after her in swarms,
but they were frightened of her. You couldn't keep up
with a tongue like she had, not running barefoot.
They used to have army coats cut down for them
all those girls, I remember;

and they used to shout till the moon was up
about plaits being a bourgeois survival.
They were savage! Oh, they used to spout.
They were always full of an idea of some sort:
for instance one might quite suddenly start
about the nationalization of babies;
of course a lot of it was ridiculous,
really harmful at times: but I'll say this –
It worries me, seeing you people,
you haven't got the drive.
The worst thing is – and you can contradict
if you want – you don't think like young people
and people are the same age as their thoughts.
There are young people, laddie, but no youth.
Well, why argue? Look at my nephew,
he won't reach twenty-five this winter,
but you wouldn't put him anywhere under thirty.
What happened? He was a boy like any other,
and you see they put him on the Committee.
He sits there, that green kid,
steamed up, banging his bossy fist –
he even walks in a different way.
There's iron in his eyes; and as for speeches,
it isn't words to get the business done,
it's business only there for the sake of words,
for smooth, obvious speeches. Well then,
what sort of a young chap's that?
What sort of enthusiasm is it?
Because it isn't "sound", you might say,
he plays no football and he's given up girls –
now he's sound. And what about the rest?

Questions? Honest disagreements?
Oh, youth isn't what it used to be.
And nor are fish: they're not the same either.'
A heavy sigh. 'Well, that's dinner finished.
Let's try a worm.'
               And he smacked his lips.
A minute later, and there he was taking
a fine great carp off his hook.
'And aren't you a fat one, eh? And there's a reward.'
He glowed with admiration and delight.
'I thought you were saying fish aren't the same?'
He looked cunning. 'Ah, but that wasn't
all of them I was talking about.'
He smiled and waved a monitory finger
as if to say, 'Bear this in mind,
that carp, brother, ended up on a hook.
I'm not proposing to end in the same way.'

Eating my aunt's wonderful soup
I found myself being stupid when talked to.
Why did the old man swim perpetually
into my mind? There are so many of them.
'I'm not your mother-in-law,' my aunt grumbled.
'Why are you so melancholy always?
Get out of it! Be simple for a change.
Come out with me and we'll look for some berries.'

Three women and two little short-haired girls
and I ...
              this piled-up lorry flying along
creaking and murmuring from field to field;
glimpses of bright-coloured machinery,

the coats of horses, corn bright pinnacles
caps handkerchiefs. We dug into the basket
and found the bread and the fresh milk for us.
From under the wheels quails shooting up like rockets,
deafening hearing, filling the ears with sound.
The world was hubbub, one great fluttering greenness.
And I lay down in the straw on one elbow
thoughtfully crumbling up a piece of bread,
and listening and watching silently.
Some boys were throwing stones beside a stream,
the sun blazed and burned, it was glowing,
but clouds were heaping up in vaporous drops,
breathing and wheezing, shifting their masses.
Everything became misty and silent.
The country people climbed into hayricks.
And suddenly and without one look back
we crashed into the downpour,
we and the downpour and the flashing lightning
careered together into the forest.
We sensibly reorganized the cart
and pulled up piles of hay to cover ourselves:
all except one. She didn't cover herself.
One of the women of forty or so,
who had sat all day staring with a fixed expression,
sat silent and eaten unsociably,
now roused herself all of a sudden, stood,
transformed into the uttermost of youth:
Oh, she was crazy, she was spirited,
she pulled the white handkerchief off her hair
and shook her shoulders, sang out loud, she sang
happy and wet through:

Barefooted through the dark forest
the berrypicker runs.
She doesn't stop for the little berries
she looks for the big ones.
She stood with her proud head looking forward
face stung with wet pine-needles, eyes shining
with tears and rain.
                        'What are you doing up there?
You fool – you'll catch your death.'
But she was giving herself entire to the rain
and the rain had given itself to her.
She threw back her hair dark-handed,
and looked into the far distance as if
she'd seen what no one else could see in it.
I thought nothing existed in the world
but this, the crowded flying lorry,
nothing existed.
                 Only the wind beating,
downpouring rain and the woman singing.
We settled into a barn to pass the night.
Under its low roof the stifling smell
of grain and dried mushrooms and wet berries.
Brooms breathed green leaves.
Between the gliding beams of light and dark
the huge horse-collars bulked under the roof
like bats.
         I couldn't sleep.
                  Texture of dark
showed faces faintly. Woman's voice. Whisper.
I strained my ears to listen.
                 'Liz, Liz,

you don't know what my life is like, you don't.
Oh, yes, we have a cactus and a Dutch
oven and a zinc roof all right:
and everything's spring-cleaned and scoured and
    polished.
and I have my husband and the children.
But haven't I a soul? It's so cruel,
so cold, and mother asks, "What's wrong with
    him?
He isn't violent, he has no secrets,
he drinks, but so does everyone drink."
Liz, he just comes home night after night
drunk, growling:
that anyway I'm his,
he turns me over roughly . . . without a word
without a word – as if I weren't a person.
Before I used to cry and not sleep,
but in the end I've found out how to sleep.
What I've turned into! . . . People think I'm forty,
and Liz, I'm only thirty-five.
What will happen to me? I've no more strength.
If only I had someone I really loved
how I'd look after him. He could beat me
if he loved me. I'd never think
of going out, I'd care for my beauty,
I'd wash his feet for him my darling,
I'd drink the water.'
                    Yes, she was the one
who flying through the rain and the wind
had sung that simple, blood-heated song.
And I the envious and credulous

had praised her for that easy thoughtlessness.
Conversation faded. Creak of the well
reached us, then it ceased. Everyone
over in the village was in bed.
Some wheels went hub-deep in the roadside mud,
chewing on it with a sated sound.
A small boy in a jacket woke us;
it was early, he had a sunburnt aggressive
nose, and a teapot in his hand.
He looked disdainfully over me and auntie
and all those sweetly asleep on the floor.
'Citizens, aren't you going out for berries?'
I don't know what you're still asleep for.'

A single cow went wandering after the rest,
a woman with no shoes was chopping wood.
A cock was crowing loudly as we passed
out of the village into wide meadows
full of the deafening din of the cicadas.
The rearing shafts of carts as still as ice,
over the earth the blue intense air.
After the open fields you come to bushes,
still cold and glistening with moisture, birds
messing about, a few wild raspberries
among the brambles soft and smoky crimson;
the whortleberries lie there to be rolled in,
pine-needles and cranberries burn your feet.
But we were after the best of the berries
the strawberries that grow in the deep woods.
Someone suddenly called out in front,
'Look there they are, and there's another lot' –

Joy of simplicity, of carrying!
The pattering of the first ones in the bucket.
But we had to submit to the young guide.
'Citizens, you just make me laugh,
we haven't got near the berries yet.'
And then a clearing broke through the trees
with a drunkenness of berries, sunlight,
and flowers, it dazzled on our eyes,
it was one breathing Oh.
The strawberries were like a waking dream
their smell was terrifying. We ran
in among them with rattling pails,
and tripped, lay there drugged, using our lips
to pluck the big berries on their stems.
On the hillocks the downy grass
hanging like smoke. The forest humming
with swarms of midges, thin humming of pines.
And I
        the strawberries dropped out of the mind,
my eyes were on that woman, watching pleasure
in all her movements taking turn with pleasure.
Her white kerchief slipped down on her forehead,
she was laughing, and picking strawberries,
and she was laughing
                I the incredulous,
and trapped by hesitation in confusion
got up out of the warm and crumpled grass
and poured my berries into someone's bucket
and wandered through the forest by no path.
From memory, no subtraction,
the calculation of remembered factors.

I came out from the pines their hollow noise
into the wheat lay shut-eyed at its feet,
and opening an eye (bird crossing sky)
sat up on the dry, stalky ground, fingered
the wheat, its ripening ears. I asked the wheat
how happiness could come for everyone.
'What can be done, wheat? Wise wheat.
Personal shame. Personal weakness.
I don't know how to set about it
I mayn't be saint enough or fitted for it.'
And the wheat answered
with head scarcely moving,
'You're neither bad nor good,
but simply very young.
It was a good question:
forgive this mute reply,
But mute comprehension
won't do to answer by.'
I followed meadow paths and tracks,
carts abandoned, whiff of tar,
met with a happy-looking fellow,
bare feet, ungodly air,
snub-nosed, covered in dust,
small, hungry, and young,
possessive with a birchwood stick
on which his boots were slung.
He talked to me with fury of
the wheat scorched where it stood
and the farm president Pankratov,
much harm and little good.
He said, 'I'm not going to take it.

I'm off. I'm for the truth;
and if they won't help at Zima,
I'm going to Irkutsk.'
Then suddenly somewhere a car appeared,
and riding in it symbol of his office
the briefcase politician in his jeep,
a man enthroned as if it were a committee.
'What's this? The hero's march on Zima?
Just mention Pankratov once again,
and you'll know it.' And he hurtled off.
There was no sober substance in the fellow,
but in the boy in his iron belief,
unmechanized, barefooted, and ungodly.
We said good-bye. He went his way, small-looking
dragging his feet rather in the dust,
boots swinging on his stick in the distance.

A few days later we were going off
one sleepy morning on a three-ton lorry
going our way. There were formal good-byes
spoken with feeling to the head of the house.
Handshakes, promises of many visits.
He was a tough, dignified old man,
a genuine Siberian lumberman.
He filled the lorry up unhurriedly
from a bucket tied with cloth to filter it.
The morning stars had faded from the sky,
under the swimming deepening blue of air
our three-tonner moved off along the road,
with the young grass still hanging from the wheels.
I won't say much about it.

Better to speak of how we all got home:
how I woke with the world
                              the drink of milk,
went off alone, the green line of the steppe,
the uncut forest on this side and that,
wandering, walking through shadows of thoughts,
treading the moving shadows of the clouds.
Sometimes I took a shot-gun into the forest,
there was no point in that, but the walking
grew pensive for me while I carried it.
I sat beneath a birch, beneath an oak,
so many meditations
                         thought of you
Uncle Volodya, Uncle Andrei,
with love.
                    Andrei's the elder
I love his sleeping, crumpled,
                                     hardly living,
the way he washes, rising very early,
the way he carries other people's children.
He runs the garage, everlastingly
enraged and smeared all over, careers
along in a van he calls the Billygoat,
with his big forehead hunched over the wheel.
His sudden quarrels, disappearances
into the country for a day or two,
and home he comes, benevolent and tired,
smelling of petrol and of virgin forest.
He likes to shake a hand until it cracks,
in fights he throws people around by twos
for amusement, does everything gaily and well,

from wood-cutting to sprinkling salt on bread.
Uncle Volodya: wonderful
the working metal seems as he grips it
shaking the woodshavings out of his hair,
and ankle-deep in the light-coloured foam:
and there's a carpenter! A carpenter!
and what a storyteller, an expert,
and often standing in the barn or sitting
on one side perched up on his joiner's bench
– about the cook who stole and who was shot
and how the fighters passed through a village
and Francesca the woman who came
from Petersburg sang the song to them.

Oh my uncles.
Oh my people.
How glorious it was until the neighbour
got at me. 'Andrei,' she said,
'and one of the drivers' wives. You could drop
a little hint to auntie. But why should you?
She knows. Volodya's a fine carpenter,
but he's a drunk, the whole town knows about it.'
She hammered at me like a woodpecker;
I ought to show some interest.
                              I didn't.
But round that time the younger of my uncles
mysteriously disappeared somewhere.
When people came the whole time wanting things
mended (toys, sofas) they were told,
'He's away for a week. Business.' Simply that,
And then the neighbour, liverishly yelling,

shoving that sharp nose in through the gate:
'Zhenka, they're ashamed in front of you:
he's laid himself out. You must learn,
my little student, you must learn from life.
Come on then.'
                        Quite radiant with evil
she took me like the mistress of the house
into the larder. There lay my uncle
fuming with vodka in his underwear,
trying to sing *Yabloko* to the wrong tune.
He saw us and half got up,
confused and sobered and sad-looking,
and said quietly, 'O Zhenka my dear,
do you understand how fond I am of you?'
I couldn't stay and watch. I was horrified,
and shocked. So I stopped eating at home,
and went off to the town café alone.

Summer's hot breathing in the town café.
At the back they were noisily slaughtering pigs.
Flash of a tray. Faces. Flypapers
hang in the windows stuck all over with flies.
The teacher blinks, fumbles with the menu,
the farm girl grumbles into the thin soup,
the woodcutter with his huge, dark arm
taps a fork on a magisterial glass.
Rather a lot of noise in the town café,
and a surging sound of flying waitresses.

Glasses of tea. In a chance conversation
we suddenly lay bare ourselves talking,

I and a man with a fat face and glasses,
quite intelligent he seemed to be.
He classed himself a Moscow journalist
writing a feature piece in Zima Junction.
I talked quite openly with him about
those first one-sided certainties,
and not unravelled knots and the profound
and intricate honesty of the hesitations.
He buying me a cranberry vodka
and gesturing away tobacco-smoke
answered, 'My dear young innocent,
I used to be just the same myself:
and always wondered what came from where,
and thinking I could manage everything,
always analysing and fighting
and trying to build a new age out of one's head.
I was brash, of course, and aggressive,
and didn't have much time for lamentations
until I needed. Later of course
I wrote my novel, it wasn't published,
and had my family. Well you have to live.
Now I'm a hack. There are a lot worse.
Took to the bottle. Disappointed they say.
Not writing now. What is he now, a writer?
He's not an influence, he's a custodian
as if his thoughts were public monuments.
Oh there are changes: but behind the speeches.
Elsewhere from what was publicly spoken
this nebulous exercise takes place:
this rumination of yesterday's silence,
and silence smothering yesterday's events.'

And in his measuring glance and his repetitions,
I could see nothing but a rage of unbelief.
Unbelief. Believing is loving.
With a pessimistic, red, fat face
he ate, lamented, smacked his lips,
well-fortified against belief or loving
by a complacent personal discontent.
'Oh hell, I was forgetting the feature piece;
I must get along to the saw-mill, time I was going.
How vile this cooking is. Well anyhow
what else could one expect. What a hole this is.'
He wiped his mouth on a paper serviette
and noticing me scowling. 'Oh yes,'
he said, 'of course this is where you come from;
I quite forget, so sorry, do excuse me.'
He muddled stupidly around
and shambled across to the door with no good-bye,
concerned neither with me nor with the others.

I paid for my indecision with interest,
wandering in the untouched forest
and listening alone to the pine-needles.

And Andrei said, 'If only I could cure you,
silly lad; come down to the club with us,
there's a concert by the Irkutsk Philharmonic.
Everyone's coming to it. Here are the tickets.
And look how crumpled up your trousers are.'
So I wandered civilly along dressed up
in a shirt that still had the heat of the iron in it,
with glorious uncles stepping it out beside me,

taking great care about their shoes, smelling
of shoe-polish, alcohol, and eau-de-Cologne.

Top of the bill was a pink-coloured torso,
Anton Bespyatnykh, Russian hero.
He did it all. Straining magnificently
he lifted a bundle of weights between his teeth,
he skipped about on sharpened cutlasses,
and did a trim little waltz on a violin,
he juggled bottles and threw balls about
and brilliantly dropped the whole lot,
he flourished inexhaustible handkerchiefs
and tied them all in one and then undid it:
embroidered with a dove with an olive branch
– the ideological climax of the show.
All the uncles applauded. 'There's a trick.'
'He's good, this fellow. Look! Look!'
And I? I too clapped a little,
otherwise I should have given offence.
Bespyatnykh bowed, exhibiting his muscles.
We went outside into the night and dark.
'Well, my boy, what did you think of it?'
But I had to have solitude for a time.
'I'm going off for a walk.' 'You hurt us you know,
the whole family's wondering about it:
you're never at home at all. Surely
it isn't a romance you're working at?'
I walked along silent and not noticed
thoughts on the ground, no soaring fantasies.
And what's a concert? Well, good luck to it!
But such a number of them I'd seen,

so very many antique performances,
with such uneconomic sycophancy
applauded pretty pictures on plates
when you couldn't get barley for soup-making;
considering the real and the unreal,
and all the metamorphosis of the truth
with the untrue, I thought also of this:
we are the guilty.
Of the miniature significant irritation,
of bodiless verses, boring, numberless
quotation and the mechanical peroration.
These long reflections ... There are two kinds of
    lovers.
One sort who cover over any offence
in flattery, who in flatteries and forgiveness
and in their longing wish obliterate it.
And after this the remorse that we nourish
so much in these our days, so long in them.
No use now for the self-blinded lover,
but for love's sight and careful, obstinate thoughts,
the exact detail and mountainous reflection
whose depth admits nothing fortuitous:
not what was great deceives or can deceive
but human falsity detracts from it.
I can neither praise what is weak nor can excuse
those who exchange the wise visions of Russia
for a conversational point. These anxious wishes
belong to the weak, their easy critical lives.
What is glorious and great for which Russia
is waiting from me is no weakness.
And courage is my wish,

in every implication of the simple fire
of single truth I shall never turn back from.
Oh everywhere, oh over the seared steppe
and the undulations of the rust-coloured sand,
over my head
                    the flags their shivering sound
staff in my hand this wood that I walk by
– conscious of nervous hesitations,
not disbeliefs but a love too violent.
In the name of truth I make these revelations
and in the name of those who have died for it.
Life not lived by the wind's emptiness.
Discriminations of the questioning reason.
Greatness in its own voice calls. Consider,
and answer equably.

So on and on these odd long wanderings:
and wooden pavements woke their clattering echoes,
houses here and there scraped their shutters,
small noisy girls ran by shouting.
'In love he said.' 'You too?' 'Do you think I'm
    dotty?'
So on and on. The mist had settled close
containing night and the night's sleeplessness,
holding hidden or suddenly revealing
a strength of engines, railways, furnaces,
dark iron mounting in the half-visible stacks.
Queer shunting-engines with prolonged funnels
moved wheezily or screamed.
Thunder of hammers.
The moving muscles of the active young

their turning shoulders, teeth, grimy faces.
Sharp and aggressive from among the wheels
the hissing steam detaching. Cold glitter
catching the track. Sides of the tenebrous engines.
Easily rolling a cigarette for a pal
flag stuck under one arm a signalman
sighed, 'Late again from Irkutsk.
Did you hear Vaska's getting a divorce?'
Then I was standing absolutely still,
peering, remembering.

> In the oil-stained coat
stepping inattentive across the rails
that chap there with the suitcase in his hand.
Not true! I thought he must have left the district;
I went close up and said in a voice like death
'I think we used to know each other once.'
And it was him! We laughed. The same Vovka!
(only no *Robinson Crusoe* in his pocket)
his lies and quarrels and those same noisy jokes,
Vovka, he must be the life of the depot.
'Can you remember our revenge on Petka?
And singing to soldiers in that hospital?
And that small girl you were going to marry?'
I wanted us to talk on and on
and to tell him everything.

> The joy and the pain.
'Vovka you're tired. You've just come off from work.'
'Oh drop all that, come down to the river.'
The path wound among night-time shadows
following shoe and boot and bare footprint
among the umbrella shapes of vegetation

and giant burdock, pewter-coloured leaves.
I was talking freely, uneasily,
and cursing quite a lot.
He listened warily, attentively,
giving no answer.
The two of us went down this small path.
There was the rottenness of the reed-beds,
the sand and smell of fish, the wet timber,
some fisherman's fire smoking. The river close.
We swam there in its black expanses.
He shouted a few words and suddenly –
forgetfulness by no deliberation,
and against expectation, memory.
Later we sat on the moon-lighted bank,
our thoughts moved in the rocking water's motion.
Somewhere not far off among the fields
horses moved in the mist. Whinny.
I thought my thought, watching the slow surface:
personal guilt.

        'You're not alone,' said Vovka,
'this is a time for all considering men.
Don't sit like that or you'll get your coat crumpled.
What a chap you are after all.
Everything's going to be discovered
and understood in the course of time,
only we have to go on thinking.
What's the hurry?' The night air moaned
with distant hooters. He got up from the ground.
'That's how it is. Well, there's work to be done;
I must get home, it's eight for me in the morning.'

It dawned.
                Everything seemed younger.
Night dissolved away to nothingness,
it got a little colder for some reason,
masses took on their authentic colour.
Some rain blew down, not enough to notice,
and he and I wandered along together.
Somewhere else, driving around,
Pankratov, complacent in his jeep,
the ponderous didactic president;
and happy with his stick of birchwood
walking among the dew's heavy sprinkle
the sly boy: stubborn, with bare feet.
Nothing exceptional. Not cold; not hot.
It was a day like any other one
but such a crowd of pigeons in the air;
I was someone good, young, going away.
I felt sad and clean
and sad perhaps because
of having learnt something
and not yet knowing what.
I drank some vodka to my friends
and strolled through Zima Junction one more time.
It was a day like any other one
the trees their brilliant shivering foliation
luminous green against the ground.
A few boys throwing rubbish at a wall,
a queue of lorries stretching, women at market
among the cows and different sorts of fruit.
And sad and free on and on
I passed the last house, climbed into the sun,

and for a long time stood on the hill-top
looking across at the station buildings
and farmhouses and barns.
And the voice of Zima Junction spoke to me
and this is what it said.
'I live quietly and crack nuts.
I gently steam with engines.
But not without reflection on these times,
these modern times, my loving meditation.
Don't worry. Yours is no unique condition,
your type of search and conflict and construction,
don't worry if you have no answer ready
to the lasting question.
Hold out, meditate, listen.
Explore. Explore. Travel the world over.
Count happiness connatural to the mind
more than truth is, and yet
no happiness to exist without it.
Walk with a cold pride
utterly ahead
wild attentive eyes
head flicked by the rain-wet
green needles of the pine,
eyelashes that shine
with tears and with thunders.
Love people.
Love entertains its own discrimination.
Have me in mind, I shall be watching.
You can return to me.
Now go.'
        I went, and I am still going.

Lies

TELLING lies to the young is wrong.
Proving to them that lies are true is wrong.
Telling them that God's in his heaven
and all's well with the world is wrong.
The young know what you mean. The young are
    people.
Tell them the difficulties can't be counted,
and let them see not only what will be
but see with clarity these present times.
Say obstacles exist they must encounter
sorrow happens, hardship happens.
The hell with it. Who never knew
the price of happiness will not be happy.
Forgive no error you recognize,
it will repeat itself, increase,
and afterwards our pupils
will not forgive in us what we forgave.

Visit

GOING to Zima Junction, quiet place.
Watching out for it in the distance
with the window of the carriage wide open,
familiar houses, ornamental carving.
The jump down from the train before it stops,
crunching along on the warm slag;
the linesman working with a hose
cursing and swearing in the stifling heat.
The ducks in midstream with their heads buried,
the perches where the poultry crow at dawn,
along the sidings ornamental stars
of white and coloured bricks set in the wall.
Walking along the dusty paving-boards,
passing the clock that sits on the town hall,
hearing behind the fence of the old market
rustle of oats and clink of weights and measures:
and there the painted wooden fruit-baskets,
the cranberries wet on the low counters,
and the bright yellow butter-balls afloat
in basins made of flower-painted china.
Same cranny where the birds are still nesting,
and, most familiar, the faded gate.
And the house is exactly the same size,
the log fence still mended with boards,
the same broom leaning upon the stove,
the same tinned mushrooms on the window-sill,
the crack in the stairs is not different,
darkening deeply down, feeding fungus. . . .
Some nut or bolt or other I'd picked up

just as I always picked something up
was clenched happily in my hand
and dropped again as I went hurrying
down to the river and the river-mist,
and wandering sometimes in the woods
by a path choked in a tangle of tall weeds
in search of some deep-coloured country flower,
and working with the freckled ferry girl,
heaving the glossy hawser hand by hand.
Trying the quality of 'old honey'
where the beehives rear up above the pond,
rocking along slow-motion in the cart,
slow rhythms of the whip's lazy flicking.
Wandering through the cranberry patches
with a casual crowd of idle lads,
and fishing beneath bridges with the noise
of trains thundering above your head,
joking, throwing your shirt off in the grass,
and diving in high from the river-bank,
with one sudden thought, how little I
have done in life, how much I can do.

Waking

WAKING then was like dreaming.
Waking then was like a lonely dream
in this cottage in this settlement,
thinking: time to go and pick mushrooms,
and ruffling your hair to wake you,
and kissing your eyes open,
all this each day a new discovery.
We stayed on at the settlement for a month,
gardens, chirping birds,
the meadow paths winding among the wheat,
tense creak of the floorboards underfoot.
And when we cut the sunflower into two
there was no need for special explanations.
When under the presentiment of dawn
we ran down into the river
(gudgeon tickle your feet in those reaches)
there was no place for complicated questions.
At first it didn't seem a mystery
incapable of human explanation
that you lay dreaming in the night beside me.
I thought it due from a just destiny
that every morning was my rendezvous
with you, which never could or would be broken.
And how I flattered myself
from time to time with proving to myself
nothing in you could be unknown to me.
You don't belong to the mind's calculations,
and you disproved each of my demonstrations,
since to be unexpected is your truth.

WAKING

You came to me never with what I knew,
never the days' familiar repetitions,
but new beginnings and your new surprise.
We felt no quarrel on that droning flight,
and yet there was a presence
moving around us circle by circle,
flying with us and measuring up to us.

The Companion

SHE was sitting on the rough embankment,
her cape too big for her tied on slapdash
over an odd little hat with a bobble on it,
her eyes brimming with tears of hopelessness.
An occasional butterfly floated down
fluttering warm wings onto the rails.
The clinkers underfoot were deep lilac.
We got cut off from our grandmothers
while the Germans were dive-bombing the train.
Katya was her name. She was nine.
I'd no idea what I could do about her,
but doubt quickly dissolved to certainty:
I'd have to take this thing under my wing;
– girls were in some sense of the word human,
a human being couldn't just be left.
The droning in the air and the explosions
receded farther into the distance,
I touched the little girl on her elbow.
'Come on. Do you hear? What are you waiting for?'
The world was big and we were not big,
and it was tough for us to walk across it.
She had galoshes on and felt boots,
I had a pair of second-hand boots.
We forded streams and tramped across the forest;
each of my feet at every step it took
taking a smaller step inside the boot.
The child was feeble, I was certain of it.
'Boo-hoo,' she'd say. 'I'm tired,' she'd say.
She'd tire in no time I was certain of it,

but as things turned out it was me who tired.
I growled I wasn't going any further
and sat down suddenly beside the fence.
'What's the matter with you?' she said.
'Don't be so stupid! Put grass in your boots.
Do you want to eat something? Why won't you talk?
Hold this tin, this is crab.
We'll have refreshments. You small boys,
you're always pretending to be brave.'
Then out I went across the prickly stubble
marching beside her in a few minutes.
Masculine pride was muttering in my mind:
I scraped together strength and I held out
for fear of what she'd say. I even whistled.
Grass was sticking out from my tattered boots.
So on and on
we walked without thinking of rest
passing craters, passing fire,
under the rocking sky of '41
tottering crazy on its smoking columns.

Weddings

THOSE weddings in wartime! The deceiving comfort!
The dishonesty of words about living.
Sonorous snowy roads.
In the wind's wicked teeth I hurry down them
to a hasty wedding at the next village.
With worn-out tread and hair down in my eyes
I go inside, I famous for my dancing,
into the noisy house.
In there tensed up with nerves and with emotion
among a crowd of friends and family,
called up, distraught, the bridegroom
sitting beside his Vera, his bride.
Will in a few days put his greatcoat on
and set out coated for the war.
Will see new country, carry a rifle.
May also drop if he is hit.
His glass is fizzing but he can't drink it.
The first night may be the last night.
And sadly eyeing me and bitter-minded
he leans in his despair across the table
and says, 'Come on then, dance.'
Drinks are forgotten. Everyone looks round.
Out I twirl to begin. Clap of my feet.
Shake.
        Scrape the floor with my toe-cap.
Whistle. Whistle. Slap hands.
Faster, leaping ceiling-high.
Moving the posters pinned up on the walls:
HITLER KAPUT

Her eyes streaming with tears.
Already soaked in sweat and out of breath –
'Dance!'
They cry out in despair, and I dance.

When I get home my feet are log-heavy:
some drunken people from another wedding
turn up behind me. Mother must let me go.
The scene again: I see it, and again
beside the edge of a trailing tablecloth
I squat down to dance.
                              She weeping
and her friends weeping. I frightened
don't feel like dancing, but you can't not dance.

On a Bicycle

UNDER the dawn I wake my two-wheel friend.
Shouting in bed my mother says to me,
'Mind you don't clatter it going downstairs!'
I walk him down he springing step to step:
those tyres he has, if you pat him flat-handed
he'll bounce your hand. I mount with an air
and as light a pair of legs as you'll encounter,
slow into Sunday ride out of the gates,
roll along asphalt, press down on the pedals,
speeding,   fearless,

   ring,

    ring,

     ring

get clear of Moscow, frighten a one-eyed cock
with a broken tail, lend a boy a spanner
(his hair a white mane) drink brown kvas
passing Kuntsevo in a cloud of dust,
lean up against the kvas tank (warmed with sun
hot on my back). The girl who's serving gives me
a handful of damp change from a damp hand,
won't say her name, 'You're artful all you boys. ...'
I smile 'So long. ...'

Riding to a cottage, to a friend, I gather
speed and swish away again on the road.
My friend unhappy whittling a big stick
beside his garage in the shining grass.
'Stolen the balls!' he says, 'infuriating!'
curses his housekeeper. 'What, my caretaker,

61

she's a good one. ...'
                     I have often seen
smiles in the background and the exchange of glances.
'How fat he is, and look at his new shoes!'
Best to be silent.
                As for you   keep walking
you things of thinness, things of bare feet,
you'll not do it, your hands will never reach.
He in his life was one who could have done.
And I observe his wide and heavy shoulders,
and undiminished by his conversation
note the preoccupation in his eyes.
He finds it hard. Better in wartime.
Life passing.
When the war was over youth was over.
'Here's the shower. Here – dry yourself.'
Walk in the forest cursing films and poems.
Then at lunch on the cool, silent terrace
sitting between my friend and my friend's wife,
drinking the long taste of the dry wine.

Soon 'Good-bye Galya', 'Good-bye Misha',
she leaning on his shoulder at the gate.
I say he'll do it. I say he will write.
But if he doesn't don't tell me about it.
Flinging along my happiness my fever,
incapable of breaking out of it,
overtaking the lorries on the road
taking each of them in a single swoop
flying behind them through cut open space
hanging on them uphill. Yes I know.

It's dangerous. I enjoy it. They hoot
and lean out and yell out,
'We'll give you a hand on the hills;
give you some speed; after that
you tear along on your own.'
Careering full tilt, pelting along
in a flurry of jokes. Turn a blind eye
to my crazy career; it's the fashion.
You can't tell me how terribly I ride.
One day I'll learn how to ride.
And I spring down at a deserted
ancient lodge by the roadside,
in dim forest light I break lilac,
twine it with ivy on to the handlebars.
Flying on, flying,
sticking my face down into dark blossom,
get into the city not quite worn out.
Switch on the lamp and switch off the light.
I put my bunch of lilac into water,
set the alarm to go at eight o'clock,
sit at the table
         write
            these lines.

Later

Oh what a sobering,
what a talking-to from conscience afterwards:
the short moment of frankness at the party
and the enemy crept up.
But to have learnt nothing is terrible,
and peering earnest eyes are terrible
detecting secret thoughts is terrible
in simple words and immature disturbance.
This diligent suspicion has no merit.
The blinded judges are no public servants.
It would be far more terrible to mistake
a friend than to mistake an enemy.

In Georgia

I LOAFED about at leisure munching pears
and bathing every morning in the sea,
drinking my khvanchkara in the bazaar,
bright shirt, felt hat; a small woman
for whom I spoilt her summer holiday.
Beneath the oleanders and beneath
the hollyhocks my boring persecutions.
A few painters wandering with palettes,
the yoghourt-seller shouting in the dawn,
and high up in the hillside restaurant
the nightfall violins scraping their strings.
From there the road struggling and weaving
and suddenly crunching on tiny stones,
twisting, rearing up, and at last
clear from the mountains and their humming voice
drops like a waterfall.
In the silent village morning
the gates playing like children,
and the old man with the silver head
leaving his piles of hay to open them.
They took us arm in arm. It was movement,
it was crisp chickens, wine a dark glimmer,
the peaches glowing softly while I ate,
emptied the horn, and dropped it on the table:
I in the Russian way dancing and weeping
to songs I am unable to translate.
She hardly trembling in her string of pearls,
lowering her shy head, the small woman
looking at me who did not know me.

Again the journey.
Among plane trees, among ivy.
Cracking green walnuts, each of us
searching with our eyes for the sea.
And I whitened my lips with pressing them,
drew my ribs tight and wept invisibly.
The coast came forward and the sea with it.

Waiting

My love will come
will fling open her arms and fold me in them,
will understand my fears, observe my changes.
In from the pouring dark, from the pitch night
without stopping to bang the taxi door
she'll run upstairs through the decaying porch
burning with love and love's happiness,
she'll run dripping upstairs, she won't knock,
will take my head in her hands,
and when she drops her overcoat on a chair,
it will slide to the floor in a blue heap.

The Knights

THEY have remained unaltered like nature,
not capable of a new inspiration,
happy to make outward renunciations
but without inward mutability.
They're in no hurry to understand,
they don't very much want to understand,
still ornamented in the idiot glitter
of old-fashioned armour, their old success.
And watching cowardice in place of courage
shoulder to shoulder in its careful ranks
I see the origin of this infection,
and trace the destiny of this obsession.
The mighty horses have worn down to tatters.
The knights are not the boys of the old days:
subject to serious infirmity,
terror of honesty, terror of battle.

Schoolmaster

THE window gives onto the white trees.
The master looks out of it at the trees,
for a long time, he looks for a long time
out through the window at the trees,
breaking his chalk slowly in one hand.
And it's only the rules of long division.
And he's forgotten the rules of long division.
Imagine not remembering long division!
A mistake on the blackboard, a mistake.
We watch him with a different attention
needing no one to hint to us about it,
there's more than difference in this attention.
The schoolmaster's wife has gone away,
we do not know where she has gone to,
we do not know why she has gone,
what we know is his wife has gone away.

His clothes are neither new nor in the fashion;
wearing the suit which he always wears
and which is neither new nor in the fashion
the master goes downstairs to the cloakroom.
He fumbles in his pocket for a ticket.
'What's the matter? Where is that ticket?
Perhaps I never picked up my ticket.
Where is the thing?' Rubbing his forehead.
'Oh, here it is. I'm getting old.
Don't argue auntie dear, I'm getting old.
You can't do much about getting old.'
We hear the door below creaking behind him.

The window gives onto the white trees.
The trees there are high and wonderful,
but they are not why we are looking out.
We look in silence at the schoolmaster.
He has a bent back and clumsy walk,
he moves without defences, clumsily,
worn out I ought to have said, clumsily.
Snow falling on him softly through silence
turns him to white under the white trees.
He whitens into white like the trees.
A little longer will make him so white
we shall not see him in the whitened trees.

Birthday

MOTHER, let me congratulate you on
the birthday of your son.
You worry so much about him. Here he lies,
he earns little, his marriage was unwise,
he's long, he's getting thin, he hasn't shaved.
Oh, what a miserable loving gaze!
I should congratulate you if I may
mother on your worry's birthday.
It was from you that he inherited
devotion without pity to this age
and arrogant and awkward in his faith
from you he took his faith, the Revolution.
You didn't make him prosperous or famous,
and fearlessness is his only talent.
Open up his windows,
let in the twittering in the leafy branches,
kiss his eyes open.
Give him his notebook and his ink bottle,
give him a drink of milk and watch him go.

Party Card

A SHOT-UP forest full of black holes.
Mind-crushing explosions.
He wants some berries, he wants some berries:
the young lieutenant, lying in his blood.
I was a smallish boy,
who crawled in the long grass till it was dark
and brought him back a cap of strawberries,
and when they came there was no use for them.
The rain of July lightly falling.
He was lying in remoteness and silence
among the ruined tanks and the dead.
The rain glistened on his eyelashes.
There were sadness and worry in his eyes.
I waited saying nothing and soaking,
like waiting for an answer to something
he couldn't answer. Passionate with silence
unable to see when he asked me,
I took his party card from his pocket.
And small and tired and without understanding
wandering in the flushed and smoking dark,
met up with refugees moving east
and somehow through the terribly flashing night
we travelled without tickets, the priest
with his long grey hair and his rucksack,
and me and a sailor with a wounded arm.
Child crying. Horse whinnying.
And answered to with love and with courage
and white, white, the bell-towers rang out
speaking to Russia with a tocsin voice.

PARTY CARD

Wheatfields blackened round their villages.
In the woman's coat I wore at that time.
I felt for the party card close to my heart.

Murder!

I CAN recall that distant valley,
the years-old rotting bridge,
the woman on the bay mare flying over
in a dark cloud of dust, pale-cheeked and graceless,
'Murder!'
She screamed it out.
I cannot lose this memory anywhere,
how people ran behind her
dropping their sickles down into the grass.
And sad and strange he was lying
over the far side of a small hill,
with an imperceptible wound under the rib,
being innocently murdered for money. . . .
I recollect the darkness of the mud,
hear the hooves,
I dream the woman in her cloud of dust.
'Murder!'
tearing my heart open.

I find it hard to live in the world,
hearing that scream, hard:
I am not yet used to human death.
I have sometimes seen, deplore it as you wish,
a spirit's imperceptible destruction.
Watching a senior comrade at his business
it terrifies me to divine his death
hardening over his face and his features.
I am not strong enough,
clench my teeth, stay silent.

MURDER!

'Murder!'
I all but scream it out.

Koshueti

I AM inside the church of Koshueti:
on a wall without dogmatic loyalty
unruly saints and questionable angels
tower upwards in front of me.
And I the savage and the unawakened
can understand hiding my awkwardness
below the painted wall of the vast church,
this picture is not part of this building –
but this building is part of this picture.
The land of Lado Gudiashvili drew
the guilty on it, not the sanctified,
neither in ridicule nor in detraction
being himself tarred with the same brush.
He was God and guilty. He was angel and devil.
Writers of poems, painters of pictures,
all we creators of the invisible change,
there are so many walls we have painted
like this one in the church at Koshueti.
We painters of icons
have had amusement from the heads of the great,
we were urbane enough to get commissions
and put a bite into their execution,
and whatever the risk and whatever
the suffering we painted faithfully
the godlike humans and the human gods.

Colours

WHEN your face
appeared over my crumpled life
at first I understood
only the poverty of what I have.
Then its particular light
on woods, on rivers, on the sea,
became my beginning in the coloured world
in which I had not yet had my beginning.
I am so frightened, I am so frightened,
of the unexpected sunrise finishing,
of revelations
and tears and the excitement finishing.
I don't fight it, my love is this fear,
I nourish it who can nourish nothing,
love's slipshod watchman.
Fear hems me in.
I am conscious that these minutes are short
and that the colours in my eyes will vanish
when your face sets.

Gentleness

THIS can't go on:
is after all injustice of its kind.
How in what year did this come into fashion?
Deliberate indifference to the living,
deliberate cultivation of the dead.
Their shoulders slump and they get drunk sometimes
and one by one they quit,
orators at the crematorium
speak words of gentleness to history.
What was it took his life from Mayakovsky?
What was it put the gun between his fingers?
If with that voice of his, with that appearance,
if ever they had offered him in life
some crumbs of gentleness.
Men live. Men are trouble-makers.
Gentleness is a posthumous honour.

Encounter

WE were sitting about taking coffee
in the aerodrome café at Copenhagen
where everything was brilliance and comfort
and stylish to the point of tedium.
The old man suddenly appeared
or rather happened like an event of nature,
in an ordinary greenish anorak
his face scarred by the salt and burning wind,
ploughing a furrow through the crowded room
and walking like a sailor from the wheel.
His beard was like the white foam of the sea
brimming and glistening around his face.
His gruffness and his winner's certainty
sent up a wave around him as he walked
through the old fashions aping modern fashions
and modern fashions aping old fashions.
He in his open collar and rough shirt
stepping aside from vermouth and pernod
stood at the bar demanding Russian vodka
and waving away soda with a 'No'.
He with the scars marking his tanned forearms
his filthy trousers and his noisy shoes
had better style than anyone in the crowd.
The solid ground seemed to quiver under
the heavy authority of that tread.
Somebody smiled across: 'Look at that!
you'd think that was Hemingway,' he said.
Expressed in details of his short gestures
and heavy motions of his fisherman's walk.

ENCOUNTER

He was a statue sketched in a rough rock,
one treading down bullets and centuries,
one walking like a man hunched in a trench,
pushing aside people and furniture.
It was the very image of Hemingway.
(Later I heard that it was Hemingway.)

Talk

YOU'RE a brave man they tell me.

                               I'm not.

Courage has never been my quality.
Only I thought it disproportionate
so to degrade myself as others did.
No foundations trembled. My voice
no more than laughed at pompous falsity;
I did no more than write, never denounced,
I left out nothing I had thought about,
defended who deserved it, put a brand
on the untalented, the ersatz writers
(doing what had anyhow to be done).
And now they press to tell me that I'm brave.
How sharply our children will be ashamed
taking at last their vengeance for these horrors
remembering how in so strange a time
common integrity could look like courage.

Babiy Yar

OVER Babiy Yar
there are no memorials.
The steep hillside like a rough inscription.
I am frightened.
Today I am as old as the Jewish race.
I seem to myself a Jew at this moment.
I, wandering in Egypt.
I, crucified. I perishing.
Even today the mark of the nails.
I think also of Dreyfus. I am he.
The Philistine my judge and my accuser.
Cut off by bars and cornered,
ringed round, spat at, lied about;
the screaming ladies with the Brussels lace
poke me in the face with parasols.
I am also a boy in Belostok,
the dropping blood spreads across the floor,
the public-bar heroes are rioting
in an equal stench of garlic and of drink.
I have no strength, go spinning from a boot,
shriek useless prayers that they don't listen to;
with a cackle of 'Thrash the kikes and save Russia!'
the corn-chandler is beating up my mother.
I seem to myself like Anna Frank
to be transparent as an April twig
and am in love, I have no need for words,
I need for us to look at one another.
How little we have to see or to smell
separated from foliage and the sky,

how much, how much in the dark room
gently embracing each other.
They're coming. Don't be afraid.
The booming and banging of the spring.
It's coming this way. Come to me.
Quickly, give me your lips.
They're battering in the door. Roar of the ice.

Over Babiy Yar
rustle of the wild grass.
The trees look threatening, look like judges.
And everything is one silent cry.
Taking my hat off
I feel myself slowly going grey.
And I am one silent cry
over the many thousands of the buried;
am every old man killed here,
every child killed here.
O my Russian people, I know you.
Your nature is international.
Foul hands rattle your clean name.
I know the goodness of my country.
How horrible it is that pompous title
the anti-semites calmly call themselves,
Society of the Russian Race.
No part of me can ever forget it.
When the last anti-semite on the earth
is buried for ever
let the International ring out.
No Jewish blood runs among my blood,
but I am as bitterly and hardly hated

by every anti-semite
as if I were a Jew. By this
I am a Russian.

People

No people are uninteresting.
Their fate is like the chronicle of planets.

Nothing in them is not particular,
and planet is dissimilar from planet.

And if a man lived in obscurity
making his friends in that obscurity
obscurity is not uninteresting.

To each his world is private,
and in that world one excellent minute.

And in that world one tragic minute.
These are private.

In any man who dies there dies with him
his first snow and kiss and fight.
It goes with him.

They are left books and bridges
and painted canvas and machinery.

Whose fate is to survive.
But what has gone is also not nothing:

by the rule of the game something has gone.
Not people die but worlds die in them.

PEOPLE

Whom we knew as faulty, the earth's creatures.
Of whom, essentially, what did we know?

Brother of a brother? Friend of friends?
Lover of lover?

We who knew our fathers
in everything, in nothing.

They perish. They cannot be brought back.
The secret worlds are not regenerated.

And every time again and again
I make my lament against destruction.

Notes on the Poems

THE poems which we chose to translate for the present anthology do not of course necessarily represent the whole of Yevtushenko's best work, though all of them happen to be favourites of the translators. Some of his finest poems would have lost so much of their meaning or vitality that it would have been hopeless to attempt any English versions. The selection deliberately tries to indicate to some degree this versatile writer's broad range of theme and mood, and even in as few as twenty-two poems it should be possible to gain a fair idea of his spontaneous variety. Since the poems were composed at different dates throughout the last decade, they also show the development of his poetic talent from precociousness to maturity.

As Yevtushenko's work is almost completely undocumented in English, we shall append some notes on the individual poems in the order in which they appear (approximately that of their composition). The original Russian titles of the poems, their dates, and other items which may be of interest are noted.

Zima Junction

'Stantsiya Zima', 1953–6. This is Yevtushenko's longest and finest poem. Though it was published only in the journal *Oktyabr* (in October 1956), it laid the basis of his fame and popularity in the Soviet Union. One episode under the title 'Berry-picking' has been reprinted subsequently in several of Yevtuskenko's books in a somewhat altered form. But generally it is, as the poet himself puts it, a fragile poem in the best sense – its various episodes complement each other, and it should be read as a whole. One may regard it as an essential commentary on Yevtushenko's whole life and poetry, and we see it as the kernel of the present volume.

Zimá (the stress is on the last vowel) is a small town in Siberia, on the trans-Siberian railway a couple of hundred miles west of Irkutsk and Lake Baikal. The name literally means 'winter'. As Yevtushenko recounts, he was brought up in Zima during the war and returned there on a visit to his relatives in the summer of 1953. This was of course one of the vital years of modern Russian history. In March Stalin died, and lay in state in the Hall of Columns in Moscow. Shortly afterwards the so-called Doctor's Plot was revealed as a fraud, and the innocent doctors were released. By the summer Beria, the mighty chief of police, had been deposed and arrested. Reference is made to all these events in the poem, which marvellously combines these weighty public themes with the poet's private sense of personal unrest. The poem is entirely autobiographical.

The passage beginning 'In 1919 at nine years old ...' refers to the Russian Civil War which followed the Bolshevik Revolution; a good deal of fighting took place in Siberia. Also a result of the Civil War are the bullet-holes mentioned in the line 'We peered out from the barn through bullet-holes'.

'Zhenka' ('Zhenya') are familiar abbreviations of the poet's name, Yevgény.

The komsomol is the Soviet Communist youth organization, whose activities are largely social.

The metrical structure of the original is fairly regular, and is based on five-foot iambic lines rhymed alternately. In our translation we have used a similar fundamental rhythm, but have treated it in a less regular, more supple manner which seems more suitable for English poetry. At several points the original takes on agile, shorter-lined rhythms reminiscent of folksong – the longest such passage is that beginning,

> And the wheat answered
> With head scarcely moving ...

We have attempted to alter the rhythms of our translation correspondingly when this occurs.

Lies
'Ne nado govorit nepravdu detyam ...', 1952.

Visit
'Soyti na tikhoy stantsii Zima ...', 1953.

Waking
'Prosnutsya bylo, kak prisnitsya ...', 1953–5. The river referred to is the Kuban, which flows through the steppe country of Krasnodár, not far from the Black Sea.

The Companion
'Sputnitsa', 1954.

Weddings
'Svadby', 1955.

On a Bicycle
'Na velosipede', 1955. Kvas is a refreshing drink, fermented but scarcely alcoholic. Kuntsevo is an industrial suburb to the south-west of Moscow.

Later
'Kakoye nastupayet otrezvlenie', 1956.

In Georgia
'Ya grushi gryz, shatalsya, volnichal ...', 1956. Khvanch-kara (stressed on the last syllable) is a sweet Georgian wine.

Waiting
'Moya lyubimaya priyedet ...', 1956.

The Knights
'Rytsari inertsii', 1956.

Schoolmaster
'Okno vykhodit v belye derevya ...', 1956. The school-master is literally a 'professor', or lecturer. (The repetitions of the original have not been exactly imitated.)

Birthday
'Pozdravlyayu vas, Mama. ...', 1956.

Party Card
'Partiny bilyet', 1957.

Murder!
'Cheloveka ubili', 1957.

Koshueti
'V tserkvi Koshueti', 1959. The church of Koshueti is a modern one, standing on the main street of Tbilisi (Tiflis), capital of Georgia. Its frescoes were executed by the most notable living Georgian artist, Lado Gudiashvili, who is said to have incurred the enmity both of the Communist party (for decorating a religious building) and of the ecclesiastical hierarchy (for his unorthodox portrayal of saints).

Colours

'Kogda vzoshlo tvoyo litso. ...', 1960.

Gentleness

'Nezhnost', *c.* 1960. 'Gentleness' is literally 'tenderness'.
The circumstances of Mayakovsky's suicide in 1930 are
still somewhat obscure.

Encounter

'Vstrecha v Kopengagene', 1960. Hemingway is one of
Yevtushenko's favourite authors.

Talk

'Razgovor'; written in New York, 1960, and thus not (as
has been claimed more than once) an answer to the critics
of 'Babiy Yar', which appeared later.

Babiy Yar

'Babiy Yar', 1961. The title is the name of a ravine near
Kiev where many thousands of Jews were massacred and
buried during the Second World War. The 'Society of the
Russian People' was a notorious organization in pre-
Revolutionary Russia, responsible for pogroms directed
against the Jews. Belostók (Polish Białystok) was formerly
part of the Russian Empire, and is nowadays included
within the frontiers of Poland.

People

'Lyudi', 1961.

In reading Russian, even to oneself, it is extremely important to know on what syllable of a word the stress falls.
Here is a list of such Russian names as occur in 'Zima

Junction' and in the shorter poems, with the stressed syllable marked by an accent.

Yevgény Yevtushénko	Mayakóvsky
Andréi	Mísha
Antón Bespyátnikh	Pankrátov
Bábiy Yar	Pétka
Baikál	Sinyávsky
Belostók	Váska
Béria	Volódya
Gálya	Vóvka
Irkútsk	Yábloko
Kátya	Zhénka
Koshuéti	Zhitómir
Kúntsevo	Zimá
Ladó Gudiashvíli	Zína

In the notes to the poems only the dates of composition and Russian titles have been given, and not bibliographical information about where the originals were published in the Soviet Union. This is partly because of incomplete data; chiefly because Yevtushenko's books and even many of the journals which have published him are virtually unobtainable in this country. However, the Russian language texts of all the poems translated in this volume can be found in *Selected Poetry of Yevtushenko* (edited by R. R. Milner-Gulland, published by the Pergamon Press, Oxford).

DATE DUE